The Mystery of the "Talking" Plants

By Howard Goodkind

Illustrated by
Jon Gampert

cpi
contemporary perspectives, inc.

This book is distributed by Silver Burdett Company, Morristown, New Jersey 07960.

Library of Congress Number: 79-16901

Art and Photo Credits

Cover Illustration by Jon Gampert
Photo on page 4, UPI.
Photos on pages 9, 32, courtesy of Cleve Backster Associates.
Photo on page 11, courtesy of the U.S. Department of the Interior.
Photo on page 17, Bruce Coleman, Inc.
Photo on page 44, David B. Cammack, Dr. Charles F. Whitehouse.
Photo on page 45, Thelma Moss.
Every effort has been made to trace the ownership of all copyrighted material in this
book and to obtain permission for its use.

Library of Congress Cataloging in Publication Data

Goodkind, Howard.
  The mystery of the "talking" plants.

  SUMMARY: Relates a variety of experiments that suggest plants make and receive
communications.
  1. Parapsychology and plants — Juvenile literature. [1. Parapsychology and plants.
2. Plants — Irritability and movements] I. Title.
  BF1045.P55G66   133.8   79-16901
  ISBN 0-89547-081-0

Manufactured in the United States of America
ISBN 0-89547-081-0

Contents

Chapter 1

An Amazing Discovery

It was a cold February morning in 1966. To most New Yorkers, it was just like any other winter day. People were going to work, to school, anywhere to keep warm. But to a man named Cleve Backster, it would be a day he would never forget.

In the next few hours, Cleve Backster would discover an almost unbelievable mystery. A green plant in Backster's office would *read his mind!*

Cleve Backster had an interesting job. He was teaching New York policemen how to use a *polygraph* — the machine we call a "lie detector." Backster was an expert at finding out whether or not people were telling the truth.

Normally Backster's office was a very busy place. His work with polygraphs was known around the world. Backster had worked for many years with the U.S. Army and the Central Intelligence Agency. But on this day in February, Backster had some free time. And looking at the plant in his office, he noticed that it needed water.

Backster watched the water go into the dry soil. He thought about this green living thing he was watering. Its name sounded important — it was a *dracaena massangeana* — but it was just a houseplant. Backster knew the plant well. Every flower shop had one.

"This plant is as alive as I am," he thought. "What would happen if I hooked its leaves to the polygraph?"

Backster knew that when a person lies — or even tries to hold back the truth — that person's heartbeat becomes faster. There are also changes in the blood pressure and the electrical properties of the skin. The person lying does not know of these changes. And no matter how calm and cool the person may seem, if he or she lies, there is no way to stop these body changes.

The polygraph records these body changes in people who are lying. Electrical connectors, called electrodes, are attached to the body of the person being questioned. As that person answers a question, the

6

polygraph records changes in blood pressure, pulse, and skin electricity. They are shown as lines on a moving sheet of paper. Trained polygraph operators, like Cleve Backster, can tell from these lines whether or not the person has lied.

As Backster looked at the plant, he wondered if a living plant might give off electrical signals just as animals and humans do.

Backster felt it might be a silly idea. But if the polygraph *did* record the plant's electrical impulses, what changes might there be as he watered the plant? Backster decided to find out.

Backster carried the plant over to a polygraph. He connected electrodes to one of the plant's larger leaves with some rubber bands. He turned on the machine. The paper began to move, and suddenly Backster became very excited. A black wavy pattern began to show on the paper. Electrical impulses *were* coming from the plant. They were seen as the same wavy lines one would find with a human subject.

Backster knew the line pattern at once. It was a "flat response" — a sign of very little electrical activity. Backster had seen those lines many times before. Now, would there be a change in those lines as he watered the plant? He reached for the watering can.

Backster guessed that if there were any change at all, it would probably start very slowly. Faster changes might show up as the water moved through the roots, stems, and then finally into the leaves. He poured the water over the soil and stepped back.

Almost at once the polygraph needle started to move quickly. There were scrawly lines all over the paper. Then the needle slowed down until it hardly moved at all. Backster was puzzled. This was exactly the opposite of what he thought was going to happen.

He looked over the long sheet of paper for an explanation. Suddenly an idea struck him. The pattern of lines looked familiar. It was like the record made by a person who is nervous at the start of a lie detector test. Backster was struck by a new question: Is it possible that a plant can become *nervous?*

Something had happened to this plant. Backster could see that in the polygraph record. But *what* had happened? And how could he find an answer? It was silly, after all, to try to compare plants with humans. A plant is nothing more than a mass of water, chlorophyll, and chemicals. How could it "feel" nervous? How could it "feel" any animal or human emotions?

Backster was suddenly happy no one had seen him doing his experiment. How could he have explained

Backster discovered that the polygraph actually showed changes in the plant's electrical impulses.

what he was doing? If anyone came into the office, he would say he was thinking of making a science fiction movie! And yet Backster knew that the polygraph couldn't be all wrong. Something had happened to that plant, and he had the proof on a piece of paper.

Chapter 2

Plants Have Feelings Too

We have all grown up with plants around us. Since we were babies, they have been as much a part of our lives as the air we breathe. The vegetables we eat are plants. The grass we walk on is made up of millions of plants tangled together into a living carpet.

Plants come in all sizes — from the very small bacteria, to the giant sequoia trees of California. Plants are a beautiful and useful part of our lives. Yet how little we really notice them from day to day.

Can you imagine that a plant could ever feel things like "fear" or "love"? There may be some people who talk to their plants once in a while, but how many would ever expect a plant to answer?

Plants range widely in size, from these giant sequoia trees found in California ... ▶

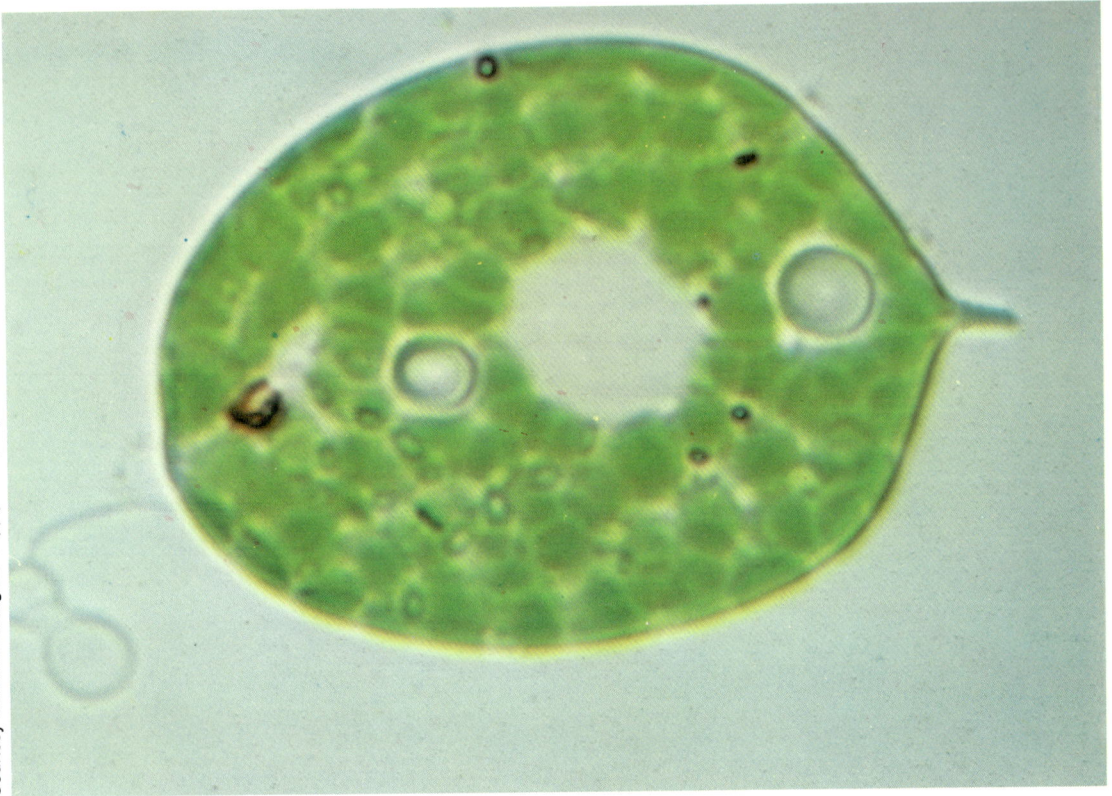

Courtesy Carolina Biological Supply Company

... to this microscopic *euglenoid* (magnified 400 times), a kind of bacterial plant that lives in the water.

Cleve Backster could not stop thinking of his experiment. Because he had worked so long with lie detectors, he knew they could record many emotions. One of these is *fear*. Could he make the plant afraid of something? Could he read that fear in a polygraph record?

Backster's eyes moved around the office. They came to rest on a cup of coffee he had just poured. Would the hot coffee do it?

12

He brought the cup over to the plant and dipped one of its leaves into the hot coffee. The polygraph reading did not change at all. No fear, no pain — just the flat response of wavy lines.

Backster tried to think of something that would be more harmful to the plant — something that might kill it. Fire. That was it! He would burn the leaves.

Before Backster had even reached for a book of matches, something happened that made his heart jump. The needle on the polygraph began to swing wildly. Backster hadn't even moved toward the plant; nothing had touched it. Yet the plant seemed suddenly "upset" about something.

Had the plant somehow felt danger? Could it know that a man was going to burn its leaves? Had this plant read Cleve Backster's mind?

Backster was really excited. He ran the experiment over and over again. He used every different plant he could find. Then he got other polygraph experts to do the same. The same thing happened for all the people who tried it. Somehow the plants were reacting to their thoughts. Somehow those plants felt that something terrible was going to happen to them.

Never again would the world be quite the same for Cleve Backster. He went on experimenting. If he could scare a plant, what would happen if he actually did burn its leaves? When he tried this he got another shock. There was almost no reaction on the polygraph. It seemed that the thought of harming the plant upset the plant more than the actual deed.

Backster thought about these results. Perhaps, he thought, by the time he had burned the leaves, it was too late to get a reading. Maybe the plants had been so afraid of what was going to happen to them that they no longer sent out many electrical signals. Perhaps they had "fainted" from all the excitement.

Once again, Backster questioned his own conclusion. Words like "faint" and "fear" are used with animals and human beings. Backster was using them now only because he did not know how else to explain the results of his experiment.

The whole idea of plants having feelings and understanding human thoughts was just too new. How could plants "feel" things the way we do? How could they possibly read our minds?

Backster knew that he had to go on with his experiments.

Chapter 3

Plants That Read the Human Mind

Following his first discoveries, Cleve Backster tried two more mind-boggling experiments. They are probably the most famous in the history of this new field of science, called plant communication.

Backster felt he had already proven that plants react to threats on their lives. Now he wanted to know if a plant could "feel" the death of some other living things. Anyone who has fed live food to fish knows the brine shrimp. It is the tiny animal you can buy at your local pet store. One cup holds thousands of them, swimming about as they look for food even smaller than themselves.

For this test Backster chose to kill tiny brine shrimp. They would not be killed, however, in the same room

Brine shrimp are so tiny that thousands fit in one cup.

as the plants. Instead, Backster's plan was to keep the plants separated from the dying shrimp.

Backster set up his experiment very carefully. He wanted to make certain that his results could only be explained in one way. Backster had become a much better researcher since his first experiment with hot coffee. If scientists were going to take his work seriously, he would have to use the same care and open-mindedness that are used in all good scientific experiments.

Backster worked with three philodendron plants. These plants are found everywhere — in homes, offices, classrooms. Backster put each plant in its own room. Temperature, moisture, and light conditions in each room were exactly the same. He connected each plant to a polygraph.

He placed the shrimp in another room with no plants in it. The shrimp were in a bowl that sat on a platform. The platform could be made to tip over from time to time. This would spill the brine shrimp into a pot of boiling water that sat on a stove below. The boiling water would kill the shrimp if they fell in.

In still another room he set up a timer that was connected to the platform. The timer would tip the

platform and spill the shrimp into the hot water. There was no way to tell when the bowl would tip and the shrimp would die. When everything was ready, Backster and his helpers left the rooms for a few hours.

When they returned they found that the platform had spilled some of the shrimp, as planned, many times. Next they looked over the polygraph records. They found that almost every time some shrimp were killed, the plants had reacted.

Some reactions were greater than others. Still, the polygraph records seemed to show a close connection between the moment of death and the plants' reactions. Can it be that the plants picked up some sort of message from the dying shrimp? If so, that message had to reach the plants *through the walls* between the rooms.

Backster noticed something else that was interesting in his shrimp experiment. After about three times, the plants' reactions became smaller. Finally they stopped altogether. The timer showed that the shrimp continued to spill from the bowl after the plants had stopped reacting. Neither Backster nor other scientists can explain why this happened.

It may be that after the same signal has been sent by the shrimp a few times, the plants can tell that they are safe. The danger signals they are picking up seem to come from a threat to something other than their own lives. They are no longer afraid.

Scientists have a great many questions about these experiments. Other scientists have tried to run Backster's shrimp experiment. Some say they have gotten the same results. Others have not. To scientists, this should not be the case. As long as the experiment is exactly the same, any scientist should be able to repeat it and get the same results.

Is it possible that in this "new science" the rules change? In studying plants it seems to matter *who* is doing the experiment. If this is true — and many good scientists say it cannot be true — we would have to believe that plants may have a kind of *ESP (extra-sensory perception)*. This would mean that plants can somehow pick up thoughts and feelings from certain people in ways we do not yet understand.

In Backster's next experiment, he tried testing the idea that plants have ESP. Could a plant somehow sense the thoughts of a human "murderer"?

Backster placed two plants in a room. One was to be murdered. The other was to be in the room at the time of the crime. Six students, without Backster watching, picked slips of paper from a hat. On one of the slips the directions for the plant murder were written. The student who picked that slip was told to take one plant out of its pot and tear it to pieces. The other students left the room while this happened. Then, after the crime, the "murderer" joined the rest of the students.

Backster returned. He attached the plant that had not been hurt to a polygraph. Then he asked the students to return one at a time. When the first five students came in, the polygraph record showed a flat response. Then the "murderer" came back to the room. The needle started to swing wildly. Had the plant — without having human or animal senses (sight, taste, touch, smell, hearing) — chosen the guilty student?

Every time Backster tried this experiment, he got the same results. But what did they mean? He couldn't explain how the plants knew one person from another — except that somehow they seemed to sense, or "remember," the murder and the "murderer."

After Backster's experiments, many scientists became more interested in the world of plants. Many of these women and men throughout the world no longer rule out the chance that plants show signs of having ESP. As more experimenting is done, it seems that plants do have more understanding of the world around them than anyone ever thought possible.

No one has yet been able to explain what this strange plant "sense" is or how it works. We are still left with only human words, like ESP, to describe the nonhuman mysteries of other living things.

Chapter 4

In Search of the "Green Thumb"

Have you ever known someone with a so-called "green thumb"? You know the type. It seems that no matter what they do, their plants are always green and strong. They tell you they don't do anything but water their plants. Yet they have the most beautiful flowers in town.

With other people, however, it is very different. They read all kinds of gardening books. But even though they follow directions perfectly, their plants never grow very well — and finally they die.

Can it be that some people just get along better with plants? Maybe they have some special talent for "communicating" with their plants. If so, does this explain why some plant researchers get better results than others?

These are interesting but very difficult questions for scientists to answer. But some scientists are trying to

do just that. Professor V.N. Pushkin of the Soviet Union is one of them. He uses hypnosis to help people make better contact with their plants. Long ago Dr. Pushkin said that he had found that plants do react to the feelings of certain people around them. Now he is trying to learn much more about how plants pick up these feelings.

In one experiment, Professor Pushkin wanted to see just how many human feelings a plant would react to. When he hypnotized his subjects, he could make them feel many different ways. For his experiment, Professor Pushkin kept plants in the room while he hypnotized his subjects. As they changed from one feeling to another, Pushkin watched the test plants to see if their reactions changed. The results were very interesting.

A student named Tanya was hypnotized. A plant was placed beside her. The plant was connected to an *encephalograph*. The encephalograph measures people's brain waves. Like the polygraph, it measures changes in electrical activity. It has been found better for studying plant response than the polygraph.

While Tanya was in a trance, she was told to feel many different ways: hot and cold; happy and sad; afraid and calm. When she was told she was cold, Tanya shivered and the plant gave a special response. When she was told she was pretty, the encephalograph showed another plant response. And so on.

26

For every different feeling that Tanya had, the plant showed a special response. Just to be sure that this was not accidental, Dr. Pushkin did the experiment over and over. He kept bringing Tanya back to the same feelings she had earlier. The plant always reacted in the same special way it had the time before. It seemed to be in close contact with every change in Tanya's mood.

Another experiment in Orangeburg, New York, showed results that were very much the same. Dr. Aristede Esser attached one polygraph to a plant and another to the plant's owner. The scientist wanted to see if they would react the same way to some questions.

Sure enough, the woman and her plant showed the same pattern on the polygraph. As the woman reacted differently to each question, so did the plant. Once again a plant seemed to feel what was on a person's mind.

Not all scientists, however, get these results in their experiments with plants and people. After their own experiments have failed, many have decided that the whole idea of plant feelings and ESP is nonsense. They compare the idea with some people's belief in flying saucers and ghosts. These might be wonderful ideas for adding fun to our lives, say these scientists, but they are not proven by real scientific study.

So there are those who believe and those who do not. This is not unusual for scientists. They argue about all kinds of ideas — the value of certain vitamins, the use of certain drugs to fight disease — a great many issues. These arguments are really very helpful. They keep us from believing new ideas too quickly, before enough time has been spent studying the question.

Because they are careful people, scientists do not jump to accept new ideas. Until everyone can get the same results in a given experiment a new idea is not thought to be proven. In every experiment *controls* are set up. For example, each time a plant's response to something is measured on a polygraph, another plant is hooked up to a polygraph as well. Everything that might affect the first plant is kept the same for the second — the temperature of the room, the sounds in the room, the light, etc. — *except* for the one thing to which the first plant will respond.

The scientist tries to rule out anything that will affect the plant other than the one response being tested.

One scientist who became interested in the new plant experiments was being very careful not to jump to any fast conclusions. Marcel Vogel was a chemist working for IBM in California. He did not believe Backster's shrimp experiment. He decided to try it for himself.

Mr. Vogel did the experiment in just the way it had been described by Backster. The plants were hooked up to polygraphs and the shrimp were killed. But nothing else happened the way it had for Backster. Mr. Vogel didn't get any reaction from his test plants at all. After trying the experiment again and getting no response, Vogel gave up. He decided he would take the plants away from the polygraph and throw them out. Lost in his own thoughts, Marcel Vogel did not notice, at first, that the polygraph needle was suddenly swinging wildly. The plants were recording a very strong reaction to something. Surprised, Vogel tried to figure out what had brought about this new response.

As far as the puzzled scientist could tell, nothing had happened to stimulate those plants. By now the swinging needle of the polygraph had slowed to the normal flat response. Vogel tried to remember when the reaction had started. It seemed to be . . . but, no, it couldn't be!

Had those plants reacted when Mr. Vogel decided to destroy them — to throw them out?

30

With that question still in mind, Marcel Vogel began his own series of experiments with plants. Today Mr. Vogel, who once had so many doubts about the reports of other plant communication scientists, is one of the top researchers in the new field of scientific plant study. His ideas are some of the brightest and most interesting in the field.

Mr. Vogel believes that plants have their own "personalities." Some plants have more feelings than others. This is why, he says, some are easier to work with on a polygraph. He says he has found that the split-leaf philodendron has more feelings than any of the other plants with which he has worked.

Vogel also makes the claim that he can "communicate" with plants. He can concentrate all of his thoughts on a plant and get responses even when he is as far as 100 miles from the plant. When he is closer, perhaps five feet from the plant, Mr. Vogel says he can do more.

Mr. Vogel thinks positive thoughts about how well the plant will grow — how strong its roots and leaves will become. Mr. Vogel feels that the plant and he are linked together as if they were lifelong friends.

Many scientists doubt that Mr. Vogel is right. His ideas are hard to believe. But the doubting smiles of many people faded not long ago. Mr. Vogel announced

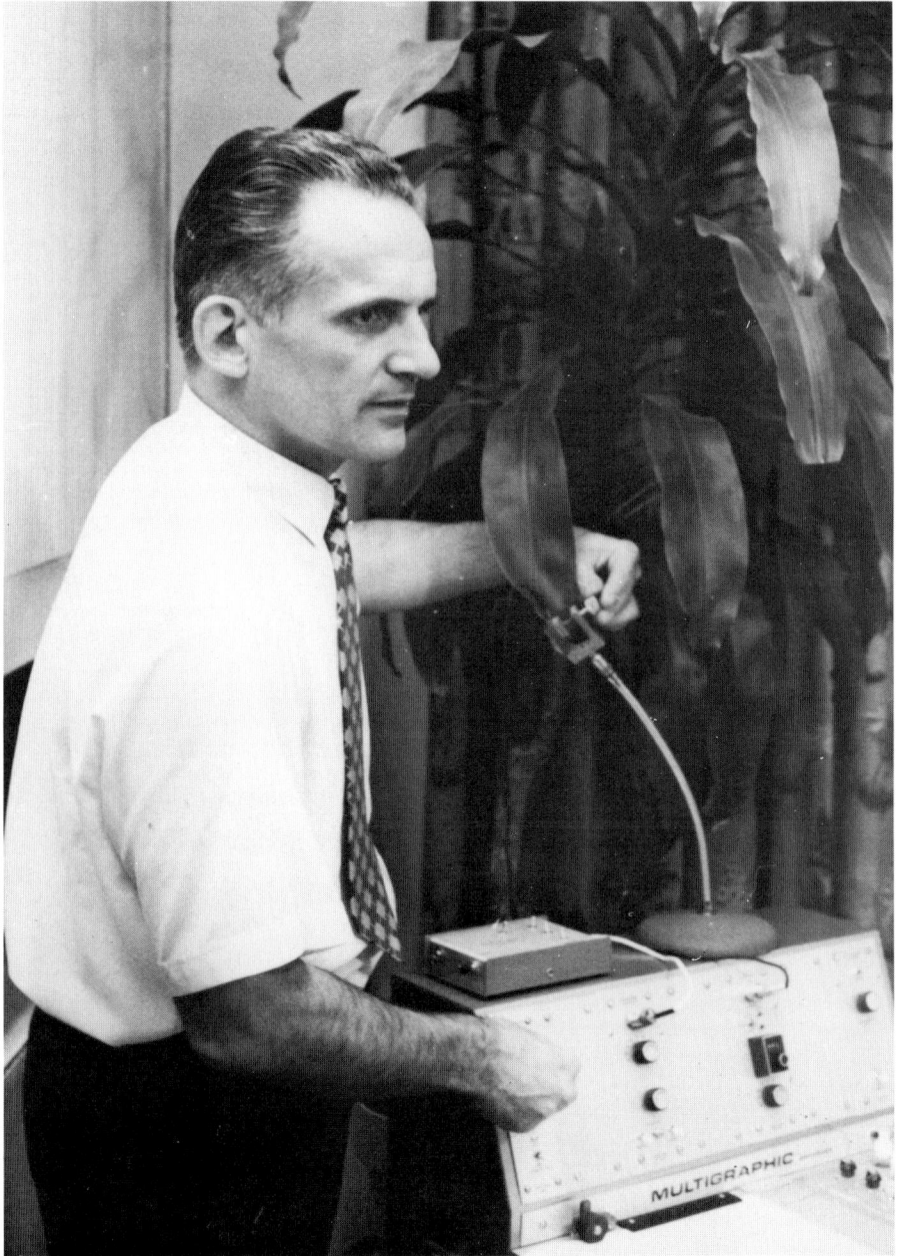

Like Marcel Vogel, Cleve Backster believes that a polygraph can record a plant's feelings.

that he had trained three other IBM scientists to do the same thing. Their concentration of thoughts let them make a special contact with their plants that they used in future testing. Of course no one claims that the reactions of these plants are exactly the same, time after time. Like the responses of all living things, Mr. Vogel believes that plants are more sensitive to stimuli at one time than another.

Mr. Vogel's work with plants goes on. As a scientist, he is not happy to stop without fully proving his ideas. But Marcel Vogel thinks his results are already successful enough to rule out mere chance.

Chapter 5

Plants and Music

Long before Cleve Backster's famous experiments in 1966, many people believed that plants were in touch with the world around them. Ancient people used to pray to their fields of crops. They would play sweet music to make them grow. Even today there are people all over the world who say their plants grow faster and stronger if they sing to them.

It is very important to some plant communication scientists to help people grow more food. They hope to help farmers grow crops quickly and more easily. More and more, plant communication is becoming an important part of that effort.

Of course there are many people besides farmers and scientists who are now interested in plant

research. Because of some newer research into the effects of sound on plants, students of music are experimenting too. Not long ago, two music students decided to experiment with the effect of music on growing plants. They made a tape recording of piano tones — five minutes of the notes *B* and *D*. They followed that with five minutes of no sounds. The tape would play over and over, without stopping, until the tape player was turned off.

The students used many plants for their test. All of them grew faster with the musical tones. African violets did well right from the start. For two weeks the experiment looked like it would be a great success. But then something strange happened.

About 14 days had passed when the geranium plants began to turn brown. They died quickly. The radishes started to bend away from the tape recorder. By the time 21 days had passed, the corn had died. Of all the plants, the only ones that kept doing well were the African violets. It seemed they loved listening to *B* and *D* tones!

The students then tried another experiment. With a new group of plants, they played an *F* tone for eight straight hours. Then they followed the tone with 16 hours of no sound. For another group of plants they played three hours of *F* tones. But they spread the playing time, stopping and starting it evenly over 24 hours. For still another group of plants, they played no musical tone at all.

After two weeks every plant that had listened to the eight straight hours of tone had died. The plants in the room with three hours of tone and many periods of no sound did best — far better than those growing without any sound. A little music seemed helpful to growing plants, but too much music was very bad for them.

Other students then joined in the experiment. They set up tape players for two different groups of plants. One tape played hard rock; the other played classical music. The classical music plants wrapped themselves around the speaker. They couldn't seem to get enough of the music. The hard-rock plants grew away from the speaker. They actually seemed to be trying to escape the music by climbing the walls.

Do plants really grow better when music they "like" is played? If they do, can't farmers grow more crops by setting up giant loudspeakers in their fields to bring plants some classical music each day?

In his book, *The Secret Power of Plants*, Brett L. Bolton talks about work in India that might lead to just that kind of farming. In the 1950s an Indian scientist,

Dr. T.C.N. Singh, did some plant experiments at Annamalai University.

Dr. Singh worked with a mimosa tree. He found that the plant grew faster and stronger when music was played to it. Seeds grew three times as fast. And as the American students discovered, Singh found that the plant died from too much music.

Under a microscope, Dr. Singh and his assistants watched plant cells. They knew that the cells were least active in the morning and the evening. These are the times they decided to try their experiments.

Dr. Singh reports that the sound of a tuning fork, held only six feet from the plants, increased the activity inside the plants' cells. And again they found that one kind of music worked better than others. But some scientists have tried to explain away Dr. Singh's results.

These scientists do not accept the idea that plant cells respond to music. Nor do they believe that any plant is made "happy" by certain music. If the plants seem to grow better with music, it is only because the sound vibrates the soil around their roots. These vibrations help the plants take in more water and chemicals from the soil. That may explain why the plants do better with sound than with no sound.

◀ Some plants seemed to like rock music best; others seemed to prefer classical music.

One of Dr. Singh's co-workers does not agree with this idea at all. She is an Indian dancer who believes that plants do "like" artistic things. She claims that plants even did better when she *danced* for them. The results from at least one experiment seem to support her.

It may be too early to judge most of these ideas about plant communication. Scientific research, after all, has only just begun. But in addition to being careful about accepting new ideas too quickly, scientists must also keep an open mind.

Do plants have the power to read our minds? Can they possibly have feelings not too different from our own? Is there some sixth sense — an extra sense called ESP in people — that helps plants to react to changes in other living things?

Do plants respond to music? Can we really believe the idea that they may even have their own personalities?

40

We know there are some who now believe these ideas. We also know there are many more who do not. But why make up your mind just yet? Why not keep an open mind until more proof is found by scientists. It may be proof that is for or against any of these ideas.

Until we have more of the facts, it is exciting just to hear about these ideas and let them work on our imaginations. That is how great discoveries are often made! That is how progress has always come about — through open-minded discovery and imagination.

Someday the ideas we hear about from plant scientists could prove very useful to us. There are already some promising new experiments going on.

Chapter 6

The Future of Plant Communication

Some plant scientists are experimenting with a new technique called *Kirlian* photography. They believe their work will lead to some discoveries about all living things.

For many years some people have believed that a blanket we cannot see surrounds all living things. This blanket is called an *aura*. This aura is a band of energy. Some people, called *psychics*, claim that they can sometimes see an aura around certain other people.

Auras, according to psychics, are always changing their color and brightness. It depends on the age and health of the living thing it surrounds. Strong and healthy people have large and glowing auras. Those who are ill, or near death, have auras with almost no color.

No one knows if there really are auras. But recently we have come close to seeing what seems to be an aura. In 1939 a Russian electrician, Semyon Kirlian, took pictures with a special camera he invented. The pictures he took showed flashes of light that appeared to shoot out from the skin of animals, plants, and people.

There is a great difference of opinion among scientists about what these pictures really show. But one thing has meaning for those interested in plants. It was found that when a part of a leaf was cut away and a Kirlian photograph made of it — *the entire leaf appeared!* And it was still surrounded by its complete aura of light.

Auras surrounded these leaves after they were picked.

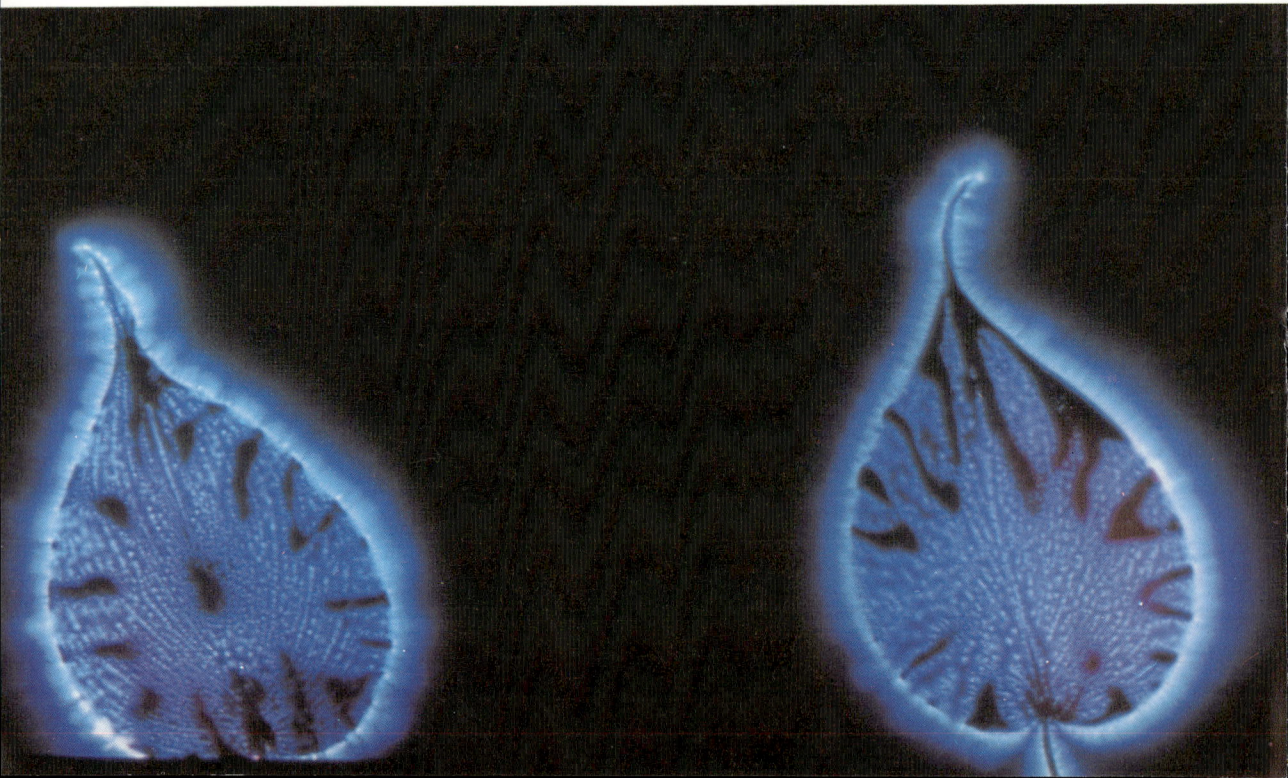

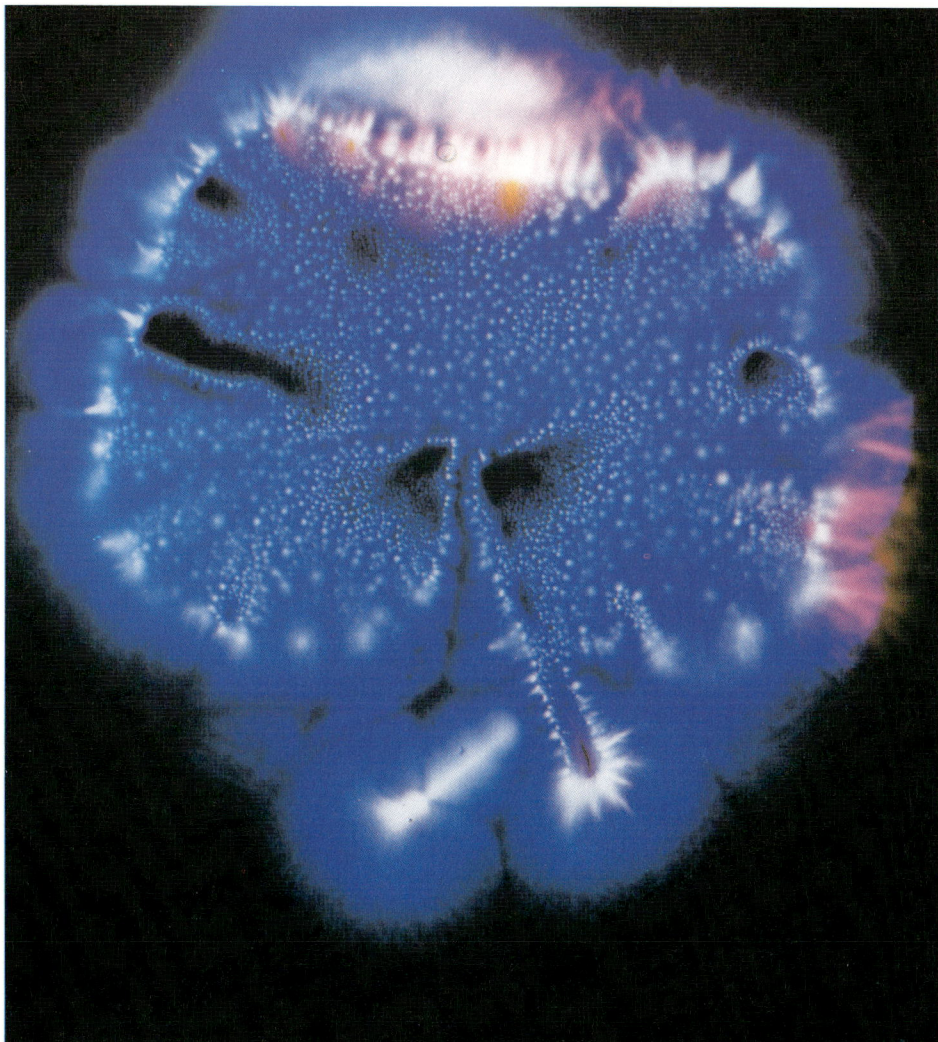

The top of this geranium leaf was removed, but the entire leaf appeared in the Kirlian photograph anyway!

This was true only if less than one third of the leaf was cut away. If more was taken off, the picture showed only what was left. Interestingly, the leaves that lost more than a third usually died right away.

People who have lost an arm or a leg often say that they can still "feel" their missing part after the operation. Is it possible that the experiments with Kirlian photographs are in some way connected to the same mystery?

In another experiment with Kirlian photographs, some researchers have had strange results. They say that someday it will be possible to rid our fields of insects without spraying with insecticides. An engineer named Curtis Upton from Princeton, New Jersey said that he had taken a picture of a field from an airplane. When he went back to his laboratory, he placed the picture on a copper plate. He then attached it to a radio transmitter. Then he put insecticide on the picture and turned on the transmitter.

After just two days, Upton says that all the insects that used to be in the field were gone. They had either died or had gone away. Somehow, he says, he had gotten rid of insects in the field from over 30 miles away.

After this, Upton tried other experiments. He photographed another field. Then he cut a corner of the picture away. He covered the rest of the picture with insecticide. Again Upton found the field free of insects in two days — except for the part of the field that had been cut away from the picture. In that part of the field he still found insects!

46

If this report is true, then why aren't farmers everywhere trying this marvelous way of getting rid of insects? Surely it is better than filling the air with deadly insecticides. Perhaps the answer is simply that scientists find it hard to believe reports that are so amazing. Or perhaps there just hasn't been enough time to test and re-test these results properly.

This is but one example of the kinds of developments we can watch for in the future. But farming is only one area that will be helped by the study of plant communication.

There is little doubt that as we understand more of how plants are able to sense and react to the world around them, we may be able to solve more of the great mysteries of nature.